A True Bird

by Maria Johnson
illustrated by Lorinda Cauley

Core Decodable 91

McGraw Hill Education

Bothell, WA • Chicago, IL • Columbus, OH • New York, NY

MHEonline.com

Copyright © 2015 McGraw-Hill Education

All rights reserved. No part of this publication may be reproduced or distributed in any form or by any means, or stored in a database or retrieval system, without the prior written consent of McGraw-Hill Education, including, but not limited to, network storage or transmission, or broadcast for distance learning.

Send all inquiries to:
McGraw-Hill Education
8787 Orion Place
Columbus, OH 43240

ISBN: 978-0-02-132394-4
MHID: 0-02-132394-1

Printed in Mexico

3 4 5 6 7 8 9 DRY 20 19 18

Sue spotted a bird.
What kind was it?
She did not have one clue.

The bird had one blue wing.
It had one ruby red wing.
Birds don't have wings like that!

And birds fly.
This one just jumped a bit.
"Is this a true bird?" asked Sue.

Sue spotted Ruth in the yard.
Ruth had a stick.

Ruth had glued a paper bird on the stick.
It was not a true bird.

"I see the truth!" yelled Sue.

"It's hard to fool you, Sue," Ruth said.